The Good in Our Hearts

A play in one act

Paul Cudenec

For Violaine in her self-searching

winteroak.org.uk

ISBN: 978-2-9575768-5-2

"The more the life of self identifies with the
life of non-self, the more intense living
becomes. The fusion of self into non-self
takes place through the more or less ritual,
conscious, or voluntary gift"

Ivan Aguéli (1869-1917)

CAST OF CHARACTERS

GEORGE: A sun-tanned, well-fed man in his late 60s. Middle-class accent.

JIM: A thin, unhealthy-looking man in his 50s. London accent.

DENISE: A woman in her 40s or 50s.

TREVORA: A heavily-built, bearded man in his 30s or 40s, dressed as a woman, wearing a wig, much make-up and false breasts. Speaks with gruff voice.

ASHOK: A man of Indian appearance and accent, in his 70s, with a long white beard and wearing a green robe.

Place

A park in central London, England.

Time

An afternoon in June.

ACT ONE AND ONLY

Setting: A large tree is flanked by two benches, placed at diagonals so that they are partly facing each other and partly facing the audience. Each is divided into three sections. Underneath the bench on the right is a heap of cardboard and newspapers. At the foot of the tree is a small triangle of green cloth.

*(enter **GEORGE**, left)*

GEORGE   Ah! Thank goodness! At last!

(sits down with evident relief on the bench on the left, placing a small suitcase beside him)

What on earth impelled me to come here? I couldn't stand the place 30 years ago, but now… I should have stayed down in Surrey, gone for a stroll in the woods, breathed some fresh air, taken my time and then popped over to the airport and flown off home. But no, I had the idiotic impulse to get up early, jump on the train and spend a few hours up here, in bloody London. What a ridiculous mistake, George! Did you really expect to find anything that would please you, that would interest you, that would feed your soul? *(sighs deeply)* Come to think of it, why did I come back at all? Yes, all right, it was my own brother's funeral but David and I never really got on and he couldn't tell from inside the coffin whether I'd turned up or not. A sense of duty, I suppose. Or of curiosity perhaps, to catch a last glimpse of that sprawling, disintegrating mess that I used to call my family. Or was it a kind of gloating, George, a sense of satisfaction at having outlived your younger brother and having had the magnificent decency to travel all the way from the south of Europe to pay your last respects? Or even of petty greed, a material revenge? Yes, yes, you know what I'm talking about! Those wine glasses! Those wine glasses that somebody gave your parents as a

wedding present – Auntie Edna
perhaps, or Uncle Reg and Aunt
Mathilda, or even Great
Grandmama herself – and which
remained untouched at the back of
the sideboard for the following
half century. Well, almost
untouched, my old fellow, because
we must never forget – how could
we ever forget or ever forgive? –
that a naughty five-year-old by the
name of George took them out of
the sideboard one rainy Sunday
afternoon, and was carefully lining
them up along the rim of the
dining table, just to take an
admiring look, when the door
suddenly opened and in his fright
he dropped the last glass, the sixth,
which shattered into fragments
seconds before the same thing
happened to his own sense of self-
esteem and security. O the shame,
how they made me feel the shame!
The glasses, too, were marked with
the shame of their inadequate
fiveness and thus condemned
never again to be removed from
their hiding place until their
owners had passed away and the

house had been sold, at which
point they fell without discussion
into the hands of little brother
David, as if the stigma of the
breaking disqualified me from
even thinking of inheriting the
remaining drinking vessels. And
indeed, yes, it was that same
lingering life-long shame that
meant I didn't even dare express
my desire to finally own the
treasure that had led me into
fateful temptation so many
decades before. So was it, I
wonder, a need to break the curse,
to confront and deflate the shame,
that made me ask David's dreary
daughter Diana if I could take the
glasses in memory of our parents,
that made me attend the funeral in
person not really because I wanted
to say goodbye to my brother but
because I wanted to get my hands
on these fetish objects that had
long for me been symbols of
innocence lost, of happiness
destroyed, of guilt, uneasiness,
hatred of myself? And now, here
they are! (*pats the suitcase*) I have
them! And what am I going to do

with them? Who knows? Put them in a cupboard, I expect, and never look at them again for the rest of my days!

(noise of a drone circling overhead)

What's that noise?

(stands up, looks around, looks up)

A drone. What's it doing? Spying on people? Why can't they leave us in peace? Everywhere you go here there are cameras. In the streets, in the tube, in the cafés and pubs and shops. They know who people are, as well, I've heard about that. They are facially recognised as they go about what used to be their private personal business, as well as being permanently tracked by the devices that they have to carry with them at all times, those little electronic gods to which they humbly bow their heads as they shuffle along with the zombie crowds.

(turns once round the tree, mimicking someone walking while looking at a phone)

Everything in this city is just so fake, so empty, so… ugly! Yes, that's the heart of the thing. It's a question of aesthetics! Cities don't *have* to be ugly, of course, even if they have always amounted to the replacement of nature by something artificial. If they are inspired by a love of beauty, of high-minded values, of some kind of sense of balance, of aspiration, of dignity, then cities can be as beautiful as the human soul at its finest. That's the kind of city we always dream of, the kind we love to visit on holiday. They're still there, all over Europe, with their cobbled streets and Gothic cathedrals, their tree-lined canals and narrow bridges, their elegant rows of houses intersected by charming archwayed passages in which we can make believe we are walking through an era other than our own. But to maintain the illusion, we have to take care not to step out of the pedestrianised area which has been so carefully preserved for our appreciation.

If we stray across the traffic-choked inner ring road which replaced the old city walls, we quickly find ourselves in a shabby zone of convenience stores, car repair workshops, hairdressers' and bus shelters. The further we travel from the beautiful centre the more we advance in time with a development of the city which cares no more for symmetry and style but only for a quick profit. Tackier and tackier become our surrounds, that's to say uglier and uglier, until we reach a concrete desert of furniture warehouses, drive-in burger restaurants, car dealers, motorway fly-overs and, beyond, a seemingly endless hinterland of chemical factories, shopping malls, pylons and airport approach roads. If we want to keep in our minds the beauty of the city centre, we have to make a conscious effort not to see all this, or not to register it, not to remember it, for otherwise the romance of Venice, Prague or Seville will be dead for us.

(stops walking, spreads arms wide)

And this place? Has London ever been a beautiful city? Not in my lifetime, for sure, but then I was born well after the German bombers did the same for our urban heritage as we did for theirs. A great opportunity to build back better, as they like to put it, with the usual inversion of meaning. London must have been ugly in a different sort of way, back in the days of soot and grime and industrial fog. They cleaned up the surface, wiped down the old buildings, put up shiny new signs everywhere, but they didn't *do away* with the ugliness, they simply *updated* it. Each decade had its own colour scheme, each palette harsher and less natural than the last, each glorying in a novelty and a modernity which are nothing but wrapping paper concealing a grotesque tumour. Do you remember, George, when you were a boy and our poor old cat was on his last legs? Every morning our mother would come down to the kitchen and find his litter tray stinking with diarrhoea and every morning, instead of opening the windows to clear the air, she would spray around a toxic substance called 'air freshener' that didn't remove the smell of cat diarrhoea but merely turned it into something even worse. I can almost taste it now, in the milk around my cereal, as we hurriedly gulped down our modern breakfast nourishment seated on modern plastic furniture under the buzz of the modern neon light. All the glitter and gaudiness in this city, all the screens and signs and shopfronts, are the visual equivalent of that chemical so-called air freshener. They can never hide the essential ugliness of London, this city built on greed and war and global theft, but simply add another nauseating layer of artifice to the age-old stink of its rotten soul. And now,

London is everywhere. Its empire of emptiness has conquered the world. Nowhere was safe from its improvements, its civilization, its development, its modernisation. And the people, too, have gradually been taken over and eaten away by that toxic plasma of spiritual emptiness, reduced to a state of grovelling obedience to the money machine, being herded on and on…

(*starts walking around the tree, head bowed, again*)

…round and round, down and down and down the plughole of existence. Next they'll let themselves be shunted into smart cities, plugged into the internet and milked of their data from cradle to grave. The whole thing is a total nightmare! We just can't go on like this! Somebody needs to *do* something!

JIM   (*speaking from within pile of cardboard under second bench*) Hear, hear!

(to George's astonishment, he emerges, brushes himself down and addresses him)

A fine speech, Sir! Of an emotional intensity fit to bring a tear to the eye of an honest working man… hypothetically, that is.

GEORGE   Err, thank you, but you see I had no idea that you were there, under the… errr…

JIM   Under the bench divided into three sections by little iron handrails, you mean? Unfortunately, *on* the bench has thus been deliberately excluded from the realm of possible repose for the weak and weary and one is therefore obliged to have a kip underneath, without the least intent of deceiving or disturbing any gentleman orators what might happen to be in the vicinity.

GEORGE   No, no, there's no question of deception or disturbance, it's merely that I imagined that I was talking solely to myself!

JIM

Of that, I was well aware, Sir, you can be sure. And, if you don't mind me saying so, what finer way of whiling away a spare five minutes than to talk out loud to oneself –

GEORGE

Well, yes, I –

JIM

(*continues and talks over him*) – especially if one likes the sound of one's own voice!

GEORGE

I wouldn't exactly say –

JIM

Personally, I can't *stand* the sound of my own voice! It never seems to have anything agreeable to say to me. It's always: 'Jim, you've only gone and fucked it up again!'. Or 'Jim, you really are an utterly useless twat!'. Or 'Jim, you do realise, don't you, that your entire life has been one miserable unmitigated failure from to start to finish?' But that's just me. I suppose if I wasn't always fucking it up, if I wasn't a useless twat and my life was a great success then my own voice would have something different to say to me and I might enjoy hearing it talking out loud to me in a public park in central London a mere few yards from a semi-slumbering ne'er-do-well? What do you say, George?

GEORGE   How do you know my —

JIM   — name? I know you are called George, George, because the lovely sound of your own mellifluous voice *addressed* yourself as George, remember? And I myself, with impressive subtlety, have just returned the favour through the indirect device of referring to the undesirability, as I feel it, of being addressed by the less-than-lovely sound of my own, somewhat harsh and hectoring voice. So the introductions have already been made. Jim has met George and George has met Jim, just to spell it out clearly in case of any momentary inattention.

GEORGE   (*laughs*) Pleased to meet you, Jim! (*instinctively reaches out to shake hands, then obviously reconsiders, only to continue the gesture in an unconvincing* *manner*)

JIM   (*waves George's hand away, half-turns from him*) No, you're right. There's no saying where it's been.

GEORGE   (*embarrassed*) Look, I'm sorry. I'm sorry for having disturbed your rest with my blathering on.

JIM   Blathering? Oh no, George, it fair tugged at the old heart strings, your poignant lament for a world despoiled by greed. I can well understand how difficult it must be for you to find yourself here, in the heart of darkness, when you have long become accustomed to living within sight of the Mediterranean.

GEORGE   Well, no, I'm not actually that close to the coast.

JIM   In your luxury villa.

GEORGE   I wouldn't say luxury.

JIM   With your large swimming pool.

GEORGE   It's quite a small one! Medium-sized, let's say.

JIM   And a bulging bank account
secured by an extremely lucrative
early period of life working in…?

GEORGE   Television. I produced comedies,
for Channel 4. Back in the early
days. Do you remember 'Pink
Spiders'? It was a cult hit. Very
popular with young people,
students. Three series, spin-off
film, stage show.

JIM   Can't say that I do, George, but
then perhaps that's because I was
never a student and thus perhaps
not fully attuned to the particular
comedic Zeitgeist that proved so
lucrative for you back in those
golden days of the 1980s, when
unemployment, spending cuts and
privatisation roll-outs went hand in
hand, mysteriously enough, with
the rise of a smart new breed of
entrepreneur whose capital was as
much cultural as financial.

GEORGE   It was a reaction *against*
Thatcherism, I would say, the
whole alternative comedy scene.

JIM　　A reaction against it that was also somehow part of it. The classic capitalist capacity for recuperation. You spit in their face and they'll sell your spittle back to you as a representation of your resistance. But listen, George, you mustn't think I hold any of this against you. I am merely musing over the vast gulf between our experiences in life which no doubt accounts for the vast gulf in our respective critiques of contemporary society. You see, George, I was very struck by the way that your objection to early 21st century capitalism, which you characterise in the form of poor old London town, is explicitly aesthetic in inspiration, even if that aesthetics is stretched to embrace the realm of odour. It is the surface that primarily offends you, even if –

GEORGE　　It's not –

JIM　　*(talks over him, waves away his abortive objection)* – even if I understand that you source what you term the ugliness to the interior of this world, to its essence. It is in the path by which you have come to your conclusions which you differ so greatly from me, George. The most harrowing memory of your childhood which you were able to muster in your compelling monologue was that of being forced to eat your breakfast in the stench of chemically-enhanced cat diarrhoea, whereas mine would be that of having no breakfast, or dinner, or tea, because I was living in the streets at the age of 12 because I hated my dad who hated his life because he was nothing and would always be nothing, just like his dad before him and the one before that and right back to the first generation of Jims who came wandering into the city in search of food and work because they had been thrown off the land by the toffs that wanted to own everything. And today, George, *your* way into understanding that all is not well with the world is a distaste for the colour of the shop fronts or an irritation regarding the way that people look at their phones when they're walking up and down, whereas *my* way of knowing this is that I sleep under bloody park benches, if I'm lucky, because I have no home, because my woman kicked me out, because I was a cunt to her, because I drank too much, just like my old man and all the other Jims before him, because I knew I was nothing and I had no job and even when I did have a job I was still nothing, and hated every minute of it, and still drank and still knew – I have always known, George, not from my head or my eyes or my nose, but from my guts, my lungs, my back, my arse! – that this world we live in is a pile of shit. It doesn't just disappoint people, George, or dismay them, or deceive them, or even destroy them, although it certainly does all that. It stops us from ever existing in the way that *you* have been able to exist. I'm just a hard shell of something that looks like a human being, full of pus and resentment – that's all you've heard from me, right? – already condemned to inevitable

nothingness generations in
advance of the day I was
unfortunate enough to be born.

GEORGE

But I don't disagree with any of
that! I can see that! You're right
that I haven't been through the
same physical misery that you
evidently have, and I'm sorry to
hear that Jim, I really am…

*(he goes to place an arm on his shoulder,
Jim backs away)*

… but that doesn't mean that I am
unaware, or uncaring. What you
are describing is the stink that I
can also smell even if, as you say,
I've discovered it by a less direct,
less material, means. That's what I
yearn for, what I'm missing, a
world ruled not by money and
power but by shared humanity,
where every single one of us can
be ourselves, live to our potential.
And I do think you're very hard on
yourself, Jim, with that inner voice
that chides you and that ridiculous
idea that you are nothing. I mean, I
have to say that I am enormously
impressed by how articulate you

are…

JIM

(*suddenly outraged*) for a dosser, right? That's what you mean? (*advances to George and pushes him in the chest, forcing him to back off*)

Oh, you're so articulate for a piece of filthy low-life! That's what you're saying isn't it? Eh? (*pushes him again*) Are you going to tell dreary Diana about me, back down in Surrey, are you? You'll have a really good laugh, won't you?

(*pushes him again. George is looking frightened. Jim now speaks with high-pitched exaggerated upper-class accent*)

Who could ever have imagined that an uncouth person such as that would be able to express himself so articulately? It's almost as if he were educated like us, almost as if he were intelligent, almost as if he had been a student and laughed along at the hilarious televisual antics of the...

(*his accent breaks down and he starts to shout*)

...pink fucking spiders who stored up great fat fucking flies of pink dosh and then pissed off to lead a pink life of Riley in the pink fucking sunshine while all the time complaining incessantly that the city they left behind them was designed in the wrong fucking colour scheme! Is that it, George?

(another push)

Is that how you look down on me from your luxury villa of high-minded values?

(grabs him by the scruff of the neck and looks as if he is going to do him violence until he notices the arrival of **DENISE***, right, at which he lets go of George. She enters running, looking behind her in some alarm, then sits on the second bench and starts tapping at her phone, evidently exchanging messages)*

JIM

(suddenly calm, sits on bench next to George's suitcase)

I'm sorry, George. That was uncalled-for. I'm revealing my lack of breeding, I'm afraid. And a deeply-ingrained self-hatred which leads me to project on to you, as a representation of the imagined superior, the condemnation of inferiority which, truth be told, is constantly being levelled against me by that inner voice which I do my best not to hear. Sit down, George, and let me make amends.

(he gestures to George's previous place on the bench. George hesitates)

Come on, please. You will accept my apology, I hope?

GEORGE Well, yes, of course. I, err…

(sits down)

JIM What do you say to a little conviviality?

(whips a bottle of red wine from a pocket of his jacket)

GEORGE Oh no, thank you very much, it's a little early for that...

JIM Now, now, come on! It's not every day that you'll be offered a glass of this! Look!

(passes bottle to George, who studies the label)

GEORGE Good grief! How on earth can you afford to buy a wine like that?

JIM *(laughs uproariously)* And there we have, encapsulated in one question, that vast gulf that separates our respective life experiences, my friend! That's definitely worth drinking to!

(produces corkscrew and opens bottle)

And now the glasses please, Sir!

GEORGE Sorry?

JIM The glasses! Unless you'd care to join me in swigging straight from the bottle, that is, but that doesn't strike me as quite being your style. And since you've already announced yourself to be in the possession of a near-complete set of wine glasses, it would seem ideal to combine our respective resources in such a way as to facilitate the civilized consumption of this rather exclusive French nectar.

GEORGE   Oh, *those* glasses. I'm not sure…
You see… But that *is* a rather fine
bottle you have… procured. Oh,
what the hell!

*(opens suitcase, rummages around to
extract glasses)*

DENISE   *(on phone)* Hi, no, he doesn't seem
to have followed me… Hope not,
anyway! Yes, sure. I think I'll stay
put for the moment, until the coast
is clear. See you in a bit. Bye!

GEORGE   Et voilà!

*(holds out glasses and Jim half-fills each.
George swills his around and sniffs at it)*

I'd let it breathe for a minute or
two. It's worth tasting at its very
best!

JIM   As you say, guv. You know, I think
you're maybe right that the two of
us are basically disturbed by the
same underlying social malady,
even if our vantage points are far
from being the same. If one man
hates a factory from the outside

because he lives nearby and it's a
blot on the landscape and another
man hates it from the inside
because he works there and it's the
blight of his life, then their hatred
is, after all, directed to one and the
same object.

GEORGE   Exactly!

JIM   Likewise, a man who has, through
birth or luck, managed to keep his
head above water and enjoy a
certain material security, but is
nevertheless aware of the
unsatisfactory nature of the society
around him, cannot really be
considered an enemy of the man
whose own bitter experience has
brought him to one and the same
conclusion.

GEORGE   Precisely that!

JIM   The ultimate injustice is that both
men are condemned to live within
a system which they consider, for
slightly different reasons, to be a
wrong-headed one, very far
separated from their notions of
how society *should* be organised.

Each man is deprived of agency to determine his own living conditions and, throughout his life, will never be offered the possibility of doing so, or of combining with other men in order to do so. Only the slightest details of social organisation are open for discussion or debate. The bulk of the thing, the overall weight that so oppresses both men, is presented to them, and inevitably accepted by them for all their criticisms, as being absolutely inevitable and unmovable. They are trapped in a prison that they might find ugly or unfair, but which for them represents nevertheless the only reality they have known or will ever know. They yearn to escape to freedom without being certain that a world outside the prison even exists, ever did exist, could exist. The men are in the prison and the prison is in the men, engrained into their deepest feeling. We are not real men, free men, but prison-men, slave-men, men who are both contained by the prison and cut

off, by the prison, from their real
selves.

GEORGE   Yes, that is very true.

JIM   What a dire situation we find
ourselves in! And it's getting worse
by the minute! The whole thing is
a total nightmare! We just can't go
on like this! Somebody needs to *do*
something!

DENISE   (*who has been listening since she finished
her call*) Oh, it must be so difficult
being a man! You poor chaps, how
you must have suffered over the
years!

JIM   I beg your pardon, Miss?

DENISE   I'm hearing a lot of talk about men
from over here. Men as slaves.
Men in prison. Men oppressed.

JIM   Above all else, Miss, you are
hearing, or overhearing perhaps,
although I suppose I should take
care not to assume too many airs
with regard to that issue, wouldn't
you say, George?

(*George shrugs*)

You are hearing a conversation, a private conversation at least in intent, in which the references to men make no claim to any universality as far as human identity is concerned, but rather refer, in an admittedly somewhat veiled manner, to the two individuals concerned, both of whom, as you may well have noticed, are men.

DENISE

Yes, don't worry, I did notice that you're men. I suppose I should be grateful that you even admit that, these days. And, as men, you talk non-stop about yourselves, about men. That's the whole problem! You seem blissfully unaware of the existence of any other kind of human being.

GEORGE

Now, Madam, I hardly think it fair to leap to such a sweeping conclusion on the basis of a few minutes of overheard conversation! In fact, before you got here, my friend Jim here…

JIM	Your friend? Why thank you, George me old mucker! I feel quite intoxicated by the precipitous rise in my social status effected by that compliment. The intoxication is definitely not down to the red wine, anyway, for which I am still awaiting the green light.
GEORGE	Yes, yes. Please don't hold back.
JIM	(*raising glass*). Chin chin! (*takes sip*)
GEORGE	What I was saying, Madam, is that, only a few minutes ago, Jim here was indeed talking about the former lady of his life with what I personally found to be a touching degree of self-criticism and empathy.
JIM	I said she kicked me out because I was a cunt to her.
DENISE	Oh yes, very touching indeed, a lovely choice of words. Cunt is a woman-thing, in case you didn't know and what you were to her was nothing to do with femininity. You got drunk and beat her up, did you Mister Man?

JIM	I wouldn't say that I exactly –
DENISE	Bullied her, did you? Pushed her around? Let her do all the work? Took her for granted? Treated her like shit? And then expected her to suck your rancid cock when you rolled back from the pub?
JIM	I think you may be confusing me with someone else, Miss. Your own dear hubbie. Or even your old dad, who knows?
DENISE	Oh no. I'm not confusing you with anyone else. I'm identifying you for what you are. And I don't have to have been a victim of child abuse or to have been married to a wife-beater to know what that is.
GEORGE	This doesn't seem fair, Madam, to pick on Jim when he has at least had the honesty to recognise that he was to blame for the breakdown of his marriage, whereas if he had never mentioned the subject to me, you would be none the wiser and would have had no ammunition with which to attack him. He's paying the price

for having been remarkably open.

DENISE	Not really, because I would have known, anyway. Like with you, you're just the same, but you would never admit it. Have you got a wife?

GEORGE	Err, not any more, she —

DENISE	I rest my case. Different social class, same gender. Pompous patriarch tramples little wifey into the dust behind closed suburban doors for year upon endless year until one day the poor thing cracks, can take no more and makes a divorce-dash for freedom. That's it, isn't it?

GEORGE	No. That's not it all. In fact, she was a rather dominating personality, was Fiona. People used to think I let her push me around. But I loved her dearly, so I let her carry on being herself and then in those final months all the gentleness behind the facade came out and… and…

	(George is crying, face buried in hands)

31

JIM	What is it, George? She died, did she, your Fiona?

(George nods)

Of some horrible disease. Cancer. Just after you headed off down to the Med for a happy retirement in the sun? Am I right?

GEORGE	Yes, that's it, yes.
DENISE	I –
JIM	*(stands up and points at Denise)* Shame on you! What a total disgrace you are! You can say what you like about me, even if it's all wrong, because at the end of the day I know that I'm not a good person and I fucking deserve to be insulted, but when you talk like that to my good friend George, the most upstanding and well-meaning gentleman you could ever hope to meet…
DENISE	I didn't know! I'm sorry, George. I didn't know your wife had died.
JIM	You didn't know, but you couldn't keep your mouth shut, could you?

You guessed. You didn't think.
You clung to your prejudices and
couldn't imagine a reality that
didn't conform to them. And look
what you've done! The man's in
tears!

DENISE   Yes, OK. I said I'm sorry. I leapt
to the wrong conclusion.

JIM   You leapt to the wrong conclusion
because you began from the wrong
premise.

DENISE   What do you mean?

JIM   You began from the assumption
that all men are the same, and that
just isn't true. Worse than that, it's
absurd. What would you think if I
said all women were the same?

DENISE   Can you tell the difference
between a man and a woman?

JIM   Well, yes, generally speaking,
although of course it's not always
possible in a particular case, such
as when –

DENISE   Fine, that's good. 'Generally
speaking'. Because that's what is

important here. We can all tell men and women apart, generally speaking, not just individually, but collectively, right? Not just in the way they look, but in the way they are. Women as a whole behave differently from men as a whole, wouldn't you agree?

JIM

I would indeed, although I was under the impression that this was something adamantly denied by the feminist tradition with which I imagine you identify.

DENISE

What do you know about feminism?

JIM

Well, I –

DENISE

Let me finish. Women in general have a way of being and men in general have a way of being. That's not to say that all women are the same or that all men are the same, but that all women share general characteristics that relate to the female gender and all men share general characteristics relating to the male gender, OK? I mean, all dogs aren't the same but we know a dog when we see one, right?

JIM

To be strictly non-sexist, I should point out that the same applies to bitches.

DENISE

I'll ignore that remark, even though it rather confirms my point about general characteristics relating to the male sex. The point I am trying to make is that there is a dog essence behind the diversity of actual dogs, in the same way that there is a tree essence behind the diversity of trees or a spider essence behind the diversity of spiders. They are not all individually the same, but they generally belong to the same essential category. Do you agree?

JIM

Yes, although I don't entirely see how —

DENISE

Don't interrupt me. Now, the human species is sexually dimorphic, meaning it has two sexes, with essential differences. One has to imagine that these two sexes evolved to be complementary, but somewhere along the line it went wrong. One sex, namely the male sex, became dominant, not just on a personal level, within relationships and families, but on a social level, meaning that male values and approaches dictated everything, while female values were marginalised and women disempowered and denigrated. This is what we call patriarchy. Are you following me?

JIM If I follow you, does that not rather imply matriarchy?

DENISE Don't be stupid. Now the trouble with a patriarchal society is that it cannot recognise itself as such. It takes its abnormal reality to be a normal one. Men, in a patriarchal society, take it for granted that they are superior to women, that they deserve to be treated with more respect, given more say, regarded as more important. And, worse still, women fall for the same nonsense. They know their place, as it were, and voluntarily step back and let men get on with running the world.

JIM	Hang on there. Couldn't that be one of those essential differences between men and women that you were talking about? That men, generally speaking, like to be in charge and women, generally speaking, are happy to let men wear the trousers, so to speak?
GEORGE	(*emerges from behind his hands*) That's not my experience! And I'm pretty sure that Fiona wasn't the only one.
DENISE	Exactly. Women don't generally like being bossed around by men, even though some put up with it. But while they might manage to avoid this on a personal level, if they are lucky, given men's expectations to the contrary, they can't avoid it on a social level. Society is not just run by men, but it's entirely based on the way men think it should be run. It's all about power and production and prestige and profit, rather than caring and communicating and cultivating and cherishing.

GEORGE	I've always thought of the pursuit of power as coming from a particular *type* of man, rather than from men in general.
DENISE	Yes, for sure. But from a particular type of *man*, not a particular type of woman. That's my point. If the influence of that particular type of man was balanced out by the influence of a particular type of woman who stood for exactly the opposite, then we wouldn't be in such a mess.
JIM	That's all well and good, but it doesn't let you off the hook for what you said to George, does it?
GEORGE	That's OK, Jim. The lady did apologise. I do see what you're saying, errr….
DENISE	Denise. Thank you George.
GEORGE	I do see what you're saying, Denise, and I suppose you must feel quite bitter at times at the way we chaps have a sort of privileged status in this world.

JIM		Oh dear. 1-0 to matriarchy.

DENISE		More like 7-1 to patriarchy, actually, but thank you, George, and it's a relief to hear you say that after what I've just been through.

JIM		Would you care for a glass of this rather classy wine, Denise? Then you can tell us exactly what experience you have been unfortunate enough to endure, presumably at the hands of one or more males of the species?

DENISE		I'd love one, thank you very much!

(George finds another glass and pours some wine into it)

I was at the Women's Freedom event down the road and we got attacked by a bunch of men who don't even know they're men, let alone that they're privileged. In the end, I was glad to get out of there in one piece, to be honest. I thought one nutter was chasing after me for a while, but I seem to have shaken him off…

(George hands her the wine)

Well, cheers!

GEORGE and **JIM**   Cheers!

DENISE   Here's for a bit of common sense in a world where everything is upside-down and back to front. You know, these days we're even being socially distanced from our own bodies, from knowing who we are. There was a speaker at the event who explained that this is all being done on purpose, as part of a global corporate agenda. Transgender quickly turns into transhuman, she said, with people turned into robots, flesh fused with artifice, blood polluted with nanotechnology. I really do despair at the state we're in and the direction we're going. The whole thing is a total nightmare! We just can't go on like this! Somebody needs to *do* something!

TREVORA   *(from back of auditorium)* Terf! I can see you! Terf! Fascist!

DENISE	Oh fuck, here he is.
	(***TREVORA*** *runs through the auditorium and mounts the stage. The others all stand up as he approaches*)
TREVORA	You can't hide from me, you know. You can't hide from the Trans Justice Squad, you filthy, oppressive terf slut!
JIM	Oi! Watch your language, mate! That's no way to talk to a lady!
TREVORA	'Mate'? You said 'mate'? Don't you dare misgender me, you Nazi! I'll have the cops onto you! And just because she's got a womb, that doesn't make her a lady.
DENISE	I haven't actually, as it turns out. I had a hysterectomy two years ago.
JIM	Just because you *haven't* got a womb, doesn't mean you're *not* a lady. In *your* case, at least, Denise.
TREVORA	And what does that mean? What are you implying? Are you suggesting that in *my* case the fact that I don't have a womb somehow disqualifies me from

being a woman?

JIM Not as such. It's more the fact that you're a man that disqualifies you from being a woman. Mate.

TREVORA *(momentarily speechless with indignation)* You're, you're, you're…

DENISE Well said, Jim. For all my dislike of testosterone-fuelled patriarchy, I do like a man with balls.

JIM I'd return the compliment and say I also like a woman with balls, if I didn't think it might give our friend here the wrong idea!

TREVORA You're… you're no friend of mine, you reactionary scumbag! That's hate speech, that is, what you just said! You can go to prison for that! Fascist! Genderist! Racist! Phobist!

(having looked on the point of exploding with anger, Trevora suddenly collapses heavily onto the ground and lies motionless)

DENISE Transphobia kills.

GEORGE *(walked over to Trevora and examines*

him) Don't say that! No, the poor thing's just fainted. I have to say I think you were both being a bit harsh on him. Her.

DENISE

Harsh on him? He wants to kill me for knowing what a woman is.

JIM

And what a woman isn't. Are you seriously taking his side, George?

GEORGE

Not entirely, no. But it seems to me that it wouldn't do any harm to *say* that he is a woman, if that's what he wants. Why go out of your way to upset him?

DENISE

So that fact that he's *not* a woman wouldn't stop you from accepting that he *is* a woman? You've got a strange relationship with the truth, George.

GEORGE

Well no, it's not a question of truth but more of politeness, for me.

JIM

Class shows again. Lying politely was ever the trademark of the British bourgeoisie.

GEORGE

It's not lying, Jim, it's adapting to somebody else's preferences. If you told me you'd rather I called you James, which I imagine is your real name, I would naturally do so. In the same way, if you wanted to be known as Jemima and referred to as 'she', I would be happy to oblige.

JIM   Jim is the name on my birth certificate. It also says I'm a male. I'll stick with that, thank you very much.

GEORGE   Of course. And I'll respect that, too. But in the case of our friend here… *(Trevora raises his head)* Ah, feeling better? I'm sorry, I don't know what you're called!

TREVORA   Trevora.

DENISE   Oh, what a pretty name!

TREVORA   Do you really think so?

(Denise exchanges glances with Jim)

DENISE   It sounds… exotic.

TREVORA   Yes, it does, doesn't it? Not like Trevor. Trevor doesn't sound exotic.

DENISE	No. Not very.
JIM	Can I ask you, Trevora, whether by any chance you were formerly known as Trevor, in a previous, less womanly, phase of your existence?
TREVORA	No, I wasn't, actually. I was called Ian. The name Trevora came to me in a dream just before I changed sex and I started using it without realising that it looks as if I used to be called Trevor and, with a total lack of imagination, just added an 'a' to the end of my dead name. People laugh at me, you know.
JIM	They don't!
TREVORA	They really do and the worst thing about it is that I have lots of imagination and that's really how I knew I was a woman in the first place!
DENISE	I don't follow.
TREVORA	When I was a boy I used to always be inventing stories about magical kingdoms and princesses and

dragons and elves and unicorns. I made books out of the stories I wrote and put on little shows for my mum, where I played all the parts myself because I was an only child, you see.

GEORGE   That sounds like great fun.

TREVORA   It was. Until my dad stopped it.

DENISE   Stopped it?

TREVORA   He came home early one afternoon. There'd been a power failure at the factory. He walked in on one of my little plays just when I was being a princess, wearing one of my mum's petticoats. He went bananas. Told my mum she was turning me into a girl. There was a horrible scene. I had to promise never to do anything like that again. The next weekend he took me up to the rec and signed me up with the under-9s football team.

DENISE   And you hated that, I suppose? I can certainly sympathise!

TREVORA   Funnily enough, I ended up loving it, mainly because I was a bit bigger than the other boys and turned out to be pretty good at football. I played centre-forward, scored loads of goals, got head-hunted and ended up an apprentice with Leyton Orient!

JIM　　So, ironically enough, you were a classic boy, in many ways? More than I ever was. I was a complete failure at sports. And, indeed, everything else, come to think of it!

TREVORA　　On the outside, yes. I was. But on the inside I felt different. I was always dreaming of fantasy worlds where people could instantly be turned into something else with nothing but the wave of a wand and a few magical words.

JIM　　I'm seeing a theme emerging here.

TREVORA　　There *was* a theme. Imagination was the theme tune of my story and gradually I realised that this meant I was really a woman.

GEORGE　　Now that's an odd thing, Trevora. Because I don't know where you got the idea from that imagination is the preserve of women! Maybe your dad and your football team weren't imaginative types, but there are plenty of boys and men who are. Famous ones, as well, all those writers, poets, composers, artists, visionaries! Take London's very own William Blake. His life and work were completely dominated by the imagination and he remained very much a man!

DENISE	George is right, you know. Men have plenty of imagination, even it usually involves imagining they know better than us women! I can see that having imagination helped you imagine yourself as a woman, but the fact that you had imagination couldn't have been the *whole* reason you thought you were really a woman, could it?

TREVORA	No. There was something else.

JIM	Do tell.

TREVORA	Well, you might think me a bit strange –

DENISE	I wouldn't let that worry you at this

stage.

TREVORA

– but I used to hang around in a cemetery, near where I worked, at lunchtime. It was just off the main road, but all lush and green – and dead quiet!

JIM

Needless to say.

TREVORA

I used to sit and think, or wander around a bit if the grass was too wet, and one day I decided to play a little game with myself. I closed my eyes (*acts all this out*) and walked slowly forward into an overgrown corner, with my hands in front of me, to see whose grave I would be led to by the guiding hand of destiny. After a few yards, I touched a tombstone, opened my eyes and saw that it was the grave of a young woman who had died a hundred years previously. Exactly a hundred years. To the day!

DENISE

Wow.

TREVORA

This really affected me. I knew I had made an important connection. I tried to tell people about it, but they all thought I was making it up. When I went back to the cemetery to look at it again, and to remember the name of the woman, I couldn't find the bloody thing. But I knew it was there! I asked myself what it meant. To start with I thought maybe she was an ancestor of mine, or a lover in a previous life, calling out to me across the century. But then I realised the truth.

GEORGE That it was you! That you were the reincarnation of the woman in the grave!

TREVORA Exactly! It was obvious! And this was the mystic moment of insight which persuaded me that I'm actually a woman. Well that, and a documentary on transitioning that I saw on BBC2.

DENISE The seed planted from above. Can I ask you a question?

TREVORA Yes. If it's not an offensive one.

DENISE If you want people to accept you as a woman, why don't you shave?

TREVORA	(*laughs*) Well, that's not so much offensive as plain daft. Because women don't shave, of course! Do you shave, errr…
DENISE	Denise. No, I don't. Not my face, anyway! I never have. And yet, somehow, I've never grown a beard. Funny, that, isn't it?
TREVORA	Some women grow beards!
DENISE	Yes, I'll grant you that. But then those women are so rare that, in the past, that fact alone would secure them a lifetime starring role in a circus freakshow, next to the midget and the two-headed sheep.
TREVORA	How dare you! How dare you call me a freak!
DENISE	No, I'm not calling *you* a freak. You are physically entirely normal. You grow a beard, when you don't shave, because you're a man. And there's nothing wrong with being a man.
JIM	Excuse me, Miss, but that's not what you were telling George and

me a few minutes ago!

GEORGE

Yes, but Denise, Jim, if our friend here, Trevora, really *feels* that he, sorry she, is a woman, beard notwithstanding…

TREVORA

Which I do!

DENISE

If I *feel* that I am the most beautiful, desirable and talented woman in the world, does that make it true?

JIM

Or if I *feel* that I have the power to fly… (*stands up on the bench*) Will that have any impact on the physical reality of gravity when I fling myself into the air? (*jumps off, lands with thud*)

TREVORA

But that's not the same! You're both talking about feeling things that obviously aren't true –

DENISE

Thanks very much!

TREVORA

– whereas I am feeling something that I *know* is true.

JIM

And you know it's true because you feel it?

TREVORA	Yes.
JIM	Your argument is impeccably circular.
GEORGE	So if I've got this right, Trevora, your identity as a woman, which you once felt calling out to you from that grave, is also the sensitive part inside you which inspires your imagination?
TREVORA	Yes, that's what it is: the inner woman, the real me trapped inside this man's body. And when I am her, I touch the depths of my soul. There was none of that when I was Ian. No magic in life. It was just work and telly, football and a pint with the lads at the weekend and then back to square one, Monday morning. Ian was an empty shell. He was never the reality; he was hiding the reality, stifling it, stopping it from blossoming.
GEORGE	Have you thought that we might in fact be dealing here with your anima?
TREVORA	My what?

DENISE	Your feminine side, that all men possess, in the same way that we women have a masculine side. Usually it gives us balance in our identity, but if it's repressed and unable to develop for some reason –
GEORGE	Such as a father who thought that imagination was for girls!
JIM	Or playing centre-forward on and off the pitch.
DENISE	– it might reassert itself in an exaggerated way, taking on a more dominant role in your character than it would naturally do.
GEORGE	The anima is also the muse, the mysterious female entity that inspires the creativity of poets and artists. It's part of us, but not all of us.
TREVORA	For you, perhaps. But for me, my identity as a woman is everything.
GEORGE	I can see that Trevora, I really can, and I am sure nobody here would want to put you back in the straitjacket of being Ian… (*Denise*

looks uncomfortable) But perhaps it would be helpful for you to think about this question of your anima, your muse, metaphorically buried for so long, and how it could be part of your newly-discovered self without the need to entirely reject your own worldly physical incarnation. You know, I think this stage of your life is just a springboard to something even greater, even better, even deeper.

TREVORA Really? That would be good news!

DENISE It certainly would.

GEORGE Let's drink to the next phase in the rebirth of your soul. Can I pour you a glass of wine, Trevora?

TREVORA Lovely, thank you. George, isn't it? *(George nods).* But only a small glass, because we women can't tolerate as much alcohol, you know!

JIM I'm not sure there's any correlation between alcohol tolerance and gender – I have had the pleasure of associating with a number of women well capable of drinking me under the proverbial table. I fancy the distinction is more to do with body size, women tending, on the whole, to be slightly smaller than the male of the species… Although obviously there are exceptions.

DENISE Some more exceptional than others.

GEORGE There you go! (*hands him glass of wine*) Here's to the flowering of the long-stifled human soul!

JIM And to the sweet scent of truth!

DENISE And to the rich, fertile soil of reality!

TREVORA Cheers! (*sits down on the bench on the right, along with Denise. George and Jim sit on the other bench*). You know, sometimes I think of how many Ians there must be out there in the world. Not just Ians, but Johns – it's the same name really, you know – and Johanns and Jeans and Juans and Gionas…

DENISE And Joans and Joannas...

TREVORA   Yes, of course. All those men and women trapped in false lives, caged up in personalities that they didn't choose for themselves, playing by the rules of a game they never agreed to take part in, living out their years doing things they don't really want to do, feeling dead inside, unfulfilled and unsatisfied without ever knowing why. And it's not their fault, it's not their individual lives that are the real problem, but this society that imprisons us, steals our real identities from us, stops us from being what we want to be, what we need to be, and then profits from our misery by pretending to be helping us, to be 'impacting' on the problems it caused! The whole thing is a total nightmare! We just can't go on like this! Somebody needs to *do* something!

(a door opens in the tree and **ASHOK** *steps out)*

ASHOK   My friends, it is I, Ashok, and I have to tell you that I have heard much wisdom here today, but

fragmented wisdom, partial
wisdom, wisdom that is not yet
wise enough to know that it is
incomplete!

*(George, Jim, Denise and Trevora look
at him with flabbergasted expressions)*

You, George, correctly identified
the fakeness, ugliness and
emptiness of this city and you, dear
Jim, so astutely dived beneath this
gawdy surface into the pit of
excrement which characterises its
social relationships. Denise was
right to identify an imbalance in
the male and female energies as a
fundamental problem in the world
of today, while nobody could fail
to be moved by the desire to live
fully one's inner and essential
identity as voiced by our friend
who is no longer the Ian he once
was, although he does not know
who he will become. And yet,
despite the illumination you have
displayed, and the common ground
you have established in the course
of your discussions, there is a
Whole to which you appear largely

ignorant and further Wholes
enclosing that Whole whose
existence you do not even suspect!

JIM Well, that's put *us* firmly in our
place.

ASHOK (*tracing a figure 8 as he walks slowly
around the two benches*). The reason
for your discontent, expressed in
such a glorious diversity of terms,
lies in the fact that many centuries
ago your civilization here in the
West embarked upon the wrong
path, the *via moderna* as they called
it at the time. Knowledge of the
Whole was discarded and the idea
of essential truth abandoned, in
favour of a flattening of thought to
the level of mere words. The soul
was sucked out of our world and
our lives and this is the sadness,
the futility that so many people feel
in their hearts in this degraded
society, the gnawing inner pain that
drives them to seek distraction,
numbness, intoxication or
destruction, of the self and of
others. This is the context in which
you are trapped and yet you do not

recognise it, since everything you think you know about the world you live in has been filtered and fed to you by those who have an interest in you remaining ignorant of your plight. Here we have the second knowledge that has been lost to you –

<table>
<tr><td>DENISE</td><td>(who has been looking impatient). I'm sorry, Mister Ashok, this is very interesting and all that but I don't remember buying a ticket for your lecture. If you've come out of your tree for a little chinwag, that's fine, but don't you think you ought to let other people get a word in edgeways?</td></tr>
<tr><td>ASHOK</td><td>(placing palms together) Of course, Madame Denise, my apologies, please do go ahead.</td></tr>
<tr><td>DENISE</td><td>Well… It's not that I've got anything in particular to say at the moment, it's more a question of principle that I don't much like being preached at by men, I mean… people… no, men in particular, actually… in the form of</td></tr>
</table>

a monologue.

ASHOK   I quite understand and you must all feel perfectly free to interrupt and contradict me in the same way as you have been so delightfully interrupting and contradicting each other up until now. Challenges and questions are the cornerstones of authentic communication. Now, as I was saying, the first knowledge lost to you is that your world is a debased one, which has taken the *via moderna* into a dead end of separation. The second knowledge lost to you is that you no longer possess the first knowledge –

JIM   Surely that's always the case, Ashok. Is it not part and parcel of the state of ignorance to be unaware of one's lack of knowledge?

ASHOK   I would not say so, Jim. If you were to suddenly find yourself in a strange city, my home town of Calcutta for instance, you would be ignorant of every aspect of that city, its streets, districts and its people, but you would be all too aware of your ignorance and of your urgent need to put that right in order to orientate yourself. If the citizens of the modern world were aware even of the possibility of something being missing from their understanding of society, their efforts to find out exactly what that something was would be like your efforts, in Calcutta, to find a street map to help you get around the city. The problem with today's modern citizens is that they think they know everything. They have been educated, they are informed, they read books and newspapers, listen to the radio, watch the television. The idea that they are fundamentally ignorant of their circumstances, and that they should thus take action to remedy this, is almost impossible for them to grasp, closing down the potential for their ignorance to be lifted. He who does not seek, cannot find. He —

DENISE and TREVORA   (*in unison*): Or she!

ASHOK (*with a smile*) He or she who does not even suspect that something has been lost, let alone know what it is, will never seek and thus can never find.

GEORGE That's very true.

ASHOK There is a further knowledge to be gained and that is that the two previous forms of ignorance have been deliberately created and are being deliberately maintained. Not only do tyrants deliberately hide from the people the truth about the condition of their lives, and deliberately hide from them the truth that this need not be the case, that a different way of living once existed and always remains possible, but they also deliberately discredit any line of argument that contradicts these lies, especially any approach that insists that these states of ignorance are deliberately imposed. And so –

TREVORA Wait a moment! I don't like where this is going! This sounds like hate-speech to me – far-right conspiracy-mongering!

ASHOK   You prove my point. The same tyrants who have hidden the truth about their situation from the people, and blinded them to any awareness that they have been dispossessed, have also conditioned large numbers of them to react angrily to any voice describing and challenging this deceit, thus creating yet another layer of mendacity and manipulation.

TREVORA   But who do you mean by 'tyrants'? Kings and queens? Aristocrats? Dictators?

ASHOK   The tyrants of today wear pin-striped suits and silk ties, rather than robes and crowns. And the principal tool of their tyranny is the monopoly of money.

TREVORA   You mean bankers, then? Global bankers?

ASHOK   They are a lot more than that, but generally speaking, yes.

TREVORA   I thought as much! You mean
Jewish bankers, don't you? You're
an anti-semitic conspiracy theorist!

JIM   He didn't say that.

GEORGE   No he didn't. It was you who
brought that in, Trevora.

ASHOK   Indeed. And why, Trevora, did you
immediately think that any
suggestion of global bankers
implied criticism of Jewish people?
Because you personally imagine
that all global bankers are Jewish?

TREVORA   Of course not! I would never say
that! I'm not anti-semitic!

ASHOK   So presumably, in that case, you
could hear criticism of global
bankers without hearing criticism
of Jewish people?

DENISE   I don't think it's as simple as that.
It's a trope, this thing about Jewish
bankers. Anti-semites, and I'm not
accusing you of anything, Ashok,
but *actual* anti-semites talk about
the crimes of global bankers and
financiers when they really mean

Jews.

JIM

And so that means that anyone, no matter how pro-Semitic they are, who casts aspersions on global bankers is automatically labelled anti-Jewish?

DENISE

Well, yes, I think that there is always that suspicion.

JIM

So it effectively becomes impossible, or illegitimate in any case, to criticise the global banking system, even though we know what enormous power it wields and what massive damage it does?

ASHOK

Quite so, and I would have gone so far as to suggest that this strange situation is itself a further layer of deliberate manipulation, were it not for the fact that this would expose me to still shriller accusations of prejudice!

TREVORA

You bet! First you tell us that when you say global bankers you don't mean Jews and then you suggest that fears of anti-semitism have been whipped up by the global bankers to stop people criticising them! Personally, I find this to be an offensive and –

DENISE

Listen. I'm Jewish. Not in a synagogue-attending way, but Jewish nonetheless. And I can see that there's big problem here, created by the bankers Ashok's talking about. A big problem for Jewish people, little Jewish people. If the bankers tell us that all criticism of global banking is anti-semitic, what they are logically saying, whether it's true or not, is that global banking is mainly Jewish. This could be a trick by non-Jewish bankers, who have put out the false idea of global bankers being mainly Jewish so that they can see off critics by labelling them anti-semitic. Or it could be *actual* Jewish bankers weaponising their Jewish identity, and our long and painful history, to discredit their enemies as anti-semitic and to call for sympathy and solidarity from other Jewish people. Either way, Jewish people like me are being used. We've got fuck all to do with the global bankers, but we're apparently supposed to stick up for them, get lumped in with them, get blamed for everything they get up to.

JIM I'd say you're being used as human shields by the bankers, whether they're Jewish or not. They pretend to be your defenders, but in truth they're your biggest enemy.

TREVORA I hadn't thought of it like that.

ASHOK Not many do, which is why the layers of lies remain largely intact. But there is a further reality I want to tell you about, beyond the deliberate hiding of truth and the taboos manufactured to reinforce that. This concerns the motivation behind these activities, the activities of the tyrants which keep the overwhelming majority of humankind trapped in the cage of modernity and ignorance. This motivation is entirely lacking in principle, in ethics, in good intentions, even *misguided* or *misplaced* good intentions. It consists entirely of self-interest, to the exclusion of all other considerations. This energy is, in itself, very dark. But when you add to this the way that it is invariably disguised with fine talk of acting in the interests of all, of fighting poverty, doing away with discrimination, helping people, saving the planet and so on, we arrive at an inversion that can only be described as a manifestation of evil. These people are not themselves evil, because they are mere human beings, but they have allowed themselves and their actions to be guided by evil and have thus become the avatars of evil on the human plane. We see this not just in their motivation and their methods, but in their physical actions: all point to death, to destruction, to dissolution. Their endless greed for quantity entails fragmentation – they break up the earth, in its natural wholeness, into separate elements which they then recombine to create sterile artifice; they tear apart communities and the natural order of human life in order to impose manufactured

societies based on individual
isolation, dependence and a
longstanding servitude which is
fast being updated to veritable
digital slavery; they fragment true
understanding, the ancient wisdom
of our forefathers – and
foremothers! – into parcels of
specialist, superficial knowledge
that serve only to accelerate the
toxic production off which they
feed. In each and every respect
their actions run counter to all that
is good and living, precisely
because they are enabling the
advance of evil. Since these tyrants
today control the structures that
run the world, we must conclude
that the world is currently ruled by
evil.

JIM   Thank you, Sir, for that uplifting
                 analysis.

DENISE   That's certainly all a bit grim.

GEORGE   Surely it's not as bad as that?

TREVORA   Are you telling us there's no hope?

ASHOK   No, not at all, my friends. Because

although evil rules the world from above, good survives below in decent, ordinary people like you, in the *hearts* of the victims of deceit even when their *heads* have been fully captured. And the good that beats within you, that flows in the blood of everything alive, in the sap of the trees and the waters of the rivers, the good of nature and reality and existence, is the force that will defeat evil. But in order to do so, it must fight the avatars of evil with avatars of good; men and women who are prepared to do the opposite to what the tyrants do. Instead of placing self-interest at the centre of our lives, we must cast it aside in the name of principle, nature, truth, beauty and freedom for all. We must *give* ourselves to good, *channel* good, *become* good to the extent that our limited human form allows. And we must live for nothing else!

JIM Well, I'd drink to that! George, dig out your last glass for the Green Prophet. Would you like a drop of this fine fluid, Sir? (*passes him bottle*)

ASHOK   What do we have here? Ah. Château Lafite Rothschild. Most appropriate, if I may say so!

(*George arrives with glass, pours some for Ashok, empties bottle by topping up others' glasses, who all stand up*)

DENISE   Here's to the forces of good!

ALL   (*raise glasses*) To good!

(*all five down their wine in one go and stand in a line holding empty glasses in front of them, continuing to speak in unison*)

Evil rules the world. Digital slavery is being imposed by the financial tyrants. The whole thing is a total nightmare! We just can't go on like this! Somebody needs to *do* something!

(*ten seconds of silence then all let go of their glasses, which smash onto the ground. Simultaneously the lights go out and/or the curtain falls*)

THE END

Also by Paul Cudenec

NON-FICTION

The Anarchist Revelation: Being What We're Meant to Be (2013)
Antibodies, Anarchangels and Other Essays (2013)
The Stifled Soul of Humankind (2014)
Forms of Freedom (2015)
Nature, Essence and Anarchy (2016)
The Green One (2017)
Fascism Rebranded: Exposing the Great Reset (2021)
The Withway: Calling Us Home (2022)
The Great Racket: The Ongoing Development of the Criminal Global System (2023)

FICTION

The Fakir of Florence: A Novel in Three Layers (2016)
No Such Place as Asha: An Extremist Novel (2019)
Enemies of the Modern World: A Triptych of Novellas (2021)

Full details at www.winteroak.org.uk. To contact Winter Oak email winteroak@greenmail.net or follow @winteroakpress on the platform previously known as Twitter.

About organic radicalism

Organic radicalism is a political philosophy which stands in direct opposition to the mindset of industrial modernity. It embraces the need for pro-active engagement in the world in order to try to bring about the far-reaching social changes which it prescribes.

It is based on the idea of a living community, Ferdinand Tonnies' *Gemeinschaft*, as opposed to the *Gesellschaft* of the capitalist state, consisting of horizontal relationships and exchanges between free human beings, rather than on sterile hierarchy.

Although inspired by the pre-industrial past, its vision is forward-looking. The drift to destruction is not inevitable – another future is possible if we can free our minds to imagine it.

More info at www.orgrad.wordpress.com

www.ingramcontent.com/pod-product-compliance
Lightning Source LLC
LaVergne TN
LVHW050927200726
843508LV00011B/2285